40

Years

In

The

Wilderness

Hunni Bunn

40 Years In The Widerness

By Hunni Bunn

ISBN:978-0-9785267-6-4

Published By:

Sandsnmyi Publishing

Formatting and Cover Design by:

Sandra N. Peoples

www.sandranpeoples.com

Dedicated to
(Big) Sammy Isley
(*father*)

In memory of
Kevin (Hank) Womack
(*nephew*)

Patrick and Tina
Gone...but not forgotten

For Mary

Don't

Don't put your hands on me
I'm not your little girl
You ain't my daddy
He's done already left this world

Love is a dangerous thing
If you don't already have it for yourself
A man can promise to give it to you
Only in the end to love you to death

His hands can make you feel good all over
Then just as quickly turn you black and blue
And in the midst of confusion
His lips will still be saying I love you

Tears slip down your weary eyes
Scared of the hurt should you tell him goodbye
Still lost in the emotion of
True love shouldn't make you cry

Raised hands once will rise again
That's just the way of the world
Until you let this kind of lovin' know
You're not his little girl

Don't hit me no more your lips should've said
The first time should have been the last
Do it ever again
And love will find out you are now my past

BEHOLD!!! He Stood At the Door and Knocked

Behold!!! He's standing at the door, knocking
Wanting to see what these thighs are stocking
The talk has sent him my way
And the talk will be the reason why he can't stay

THE TALK

They be praising
The way my hips be swaying
Whispering sweet nothings in my ear
Because they know they won't be staying
But only for one night
To feel how the juices flow
They only want to treasure me
Long enough to run and tell so-and-so
That honey sure was sweet
In fact, it was almost scary
For if her lifestyle came with a different label
We surely would one day marry
But too many men have been there
And no virtue between her legs doth lie
As much as I'd like to have stayed
I had to tell her goodbye

TALK FROM WITHIN

And I take delight in
I'll be seeing him again
For I am like Lay's chips
When it comes to what is between these hips
One time will never be enough
When it comes to my mushy gushy stuff
But too many pickers have taken from this apple tree
In order to grow again I must tell them to flee
So, I take down my sign
In order to allow my heart and mental to align
Seeking what I already know to be true
The love I need for myself is not in you, you or you

TALK OVER

Behold!!! He stands at the door, knocking
Unaware of the fact, my wares I am no longer hocking
I deserve so much more
Than that false love on the other side of the door

For My Little Diva

Let me go ahead and get
What I know this world is going to steal
For innocence of youth and time
Can never come as a packaged deal
Life is going to rob you of many things
First to go will be your sight
For it's going to paint a beautiful picture
Of what's wrong and what's right
Right will begin to fade to black-and-white
The beauty of it will only be seen as hindsight
But wrong will dance before your very eyes
As being the desired prize
And you'll reach out for it
Even knowing it may bring about your demise
It will sprinkle you with lust
And have you believing it's true love
Only to be doused in the afterthoughts
That come with what could I've been thinking of
Oh yes, the ride will become painful
Filled with much understanding as heartbreak
But, in reality, life will never give you
More than what your mind can take
Still, you'll have to play the cards you've been dealt
By this cold cruel world
That's why, while you are still mommy's little baby
Let me wrap my arms around my little girl

Story Has It

Story has it
You've always been spoiled
Like a rotten potato
Someone forgot to boil

Story has it
You've always had it good
Parents gave you the best
Whenever they could

Story has it
You've always sat on your behind
Never had a worry
As long as they stayed on their grind

Story has it
You were in and out the door
Carrying on like you never had any raisin'
In other words, just a common street whore

Story has it
All you are doing is waiting for them to die
Gone have that check in your hand
Before you can even tell them a proper goodbye

Well, story is
I was never spoiled
Had a childhood
Filled with much turmoil

Story is
There were many bitter days for me
A prisoner in my own home
It was through reading that I ran free

Story is
I cashed many checks in my name
Might not amounted to much
But they kept me in the game

Story is
The streets didn't care where I came from
As long as I could hold my own
I was always welcomed

Story is
I can't miss what I never had
So, the next time someone tries to tell my story
Tell them for me…enough said…

You're Worthy

Trampled by many feet
Feeling lower than low
Everybody is pushing you further away
From where you need to go
They don't care to see you make it
Want to see you get to the place where you can't take
it
But have strength to endure
And when all else fails; prayer is the cure

You're worthy
Of living this life you've been given
You're worthy
Of every minute and GOD wants you in it
You're worthy
Of all your time even if you ain't got one thin dime
You're worthy

Nobody seems to understand
That the playing field has always been even
Because one thing is for sure
If you are born then one day you will be leavin'
Even though others may flex
Ain't no one better than the next
Judgment day has been designed
For those who've gone on and those who've been left
behind

You're worthy
Of living this life you've been given
You're worthy
Of every minute and GOD wants you in it
You're worthy
Of all your time even if you ain't got one thin dime
You're worthy

Your life might be riddled
With a lot of hurt and pain
You might try your hardest
And still nothing more is gained
Trials and tribulations
Might be gripping your very foundation
Still your life has a reason
And every day begins a new season

You're worthy
Of living this life you've been given
You're worthy
Of every minute and GOD wants you in it
You're worthy
Of all your time even if you ain't got one thin dime
You're worthy

Life Ain't Living

Running full steam ahead
Always in the wrong direction
When asked to be seated
Always choosing the wrong section
You simply can't get the hang of
Where you are suppose to be
See, you may be grown
But, you still ain't free
Society still has you by the hand
Dictating who you ought to be
For your goals and aspirations
Should be built around the economy
You can choose to be a dreamer
If that's what you want to be
But, for most who dream
Will eventually wake up to a cruel reality
Bills due before they even hit the mailbox
And they must be paid
If you are to be able
To lie in the bed you made
So, put happiness on the back burner
If you are to have a life
Or go chasing your dreams
And enjoy living regardless of the strife

Hunni Bunn

I'm Not For Sale

Bills yet to be paid
In places where I've laid
Sometimes without a bed
Or a pillow to rest my head
Looking for a place of peace
Without having to be deceased
Adding to an expense
That already has me tense

Still, I'm not for sale
There's no price owed to hell
That's why I'm not for sale
I'm paying the cost every time I fail
Still, I'm not for sale

The I-owe-yous keep mounting
While I'm no longer counting
Too many debts to attest to
Gave my all to you
Even when I didn't have a penny to my name
I helped to keep you in the game
Now you are pointing fingers
Since my debts seem to linger

Still, I'm not for sale
There's no price owed to hell
That's why I'm not for sale
I'm paying the cost every time I fail
Still, I'm not for sale

40 Years in the Wilderness

The cost has been added up
Because the world is so corrupt
Want to put a price on everything
No matter what my heart may bring
In easing the pain of others
In trying to love one another
But the good of my works are dead
If your pockets are not being fed

Still, I'm not for sale
There's no price owed to hell
That's why I'm not for sale
I'm paying the cost every time I fail
Still, I'm not for sale

Don't Forget to Stay

My heart is heavy
Now that you are saying bye to me
But there's something about loving you
And my heart is telling me it's time to set you free
Maybe for a moment
Maybe even a lifetime
But to bottle you up for myself
Would sure enough be a crime

Too good to be with just me
So I'm sending you on your way
And if you should find yourself here again
Don't forget to stay

When it comes to the heart
Some men are just too strong
And to one woman
They should never belong
I only have one GOD
To whom I should bow
But this man done got a hold of me
And to release him, I don't know how

Too good to be with just me
So I'm sending you on your way
And if you should find yourself here again
Don't forget to stay

His loving so good
My heart will ache

40 Years in the Wilderness

Long before he'll ever say goodbye
Always anticipating the heartbreak
That some other woman
Will want the smile behind my eyes
And will work on a master plan
In getting YOU to tell me goodbye

Too good to be with just me
So I'm sending you on your way
And if you should find yourself here again
Don't forget to stay

Behind Closed Doors

He loves her…
I hear the whispers
As we walk hand-in-hand
Watching eyes that will never understand
Loving and so understanding
They'll never understand his loving is so demanding
Always on my p's and q's
Always paying love my dues
To say at least I got a man
Because that's always been society's plan
Even if he rules me with a firm hand
No, they will never see
The hand that love has dealt me
A game full of pass the blame
With speeches riddled with women are all the same
Ho, fix me something to eat
Rise against me and get knocked off your feet
Without me, you are nothing at all
So, go ahead and give your girls a call
They'll tell you how good you have it
Because you have the shoes they wish they could fit
They wish they had a man
So, you should be happy from where they stand
So, I accept love's token
From a man who's left me broken
The I love yous
Will never yield clues
For only love knows the true score
As to what goes on behind closed doors

You Don't Know My Walk

Did you know the hurt
Behind her eyes
Were you there when the men without invitations
Invited themselves between her thighs
Did you hear the investigator
When he told her it was all lies
It's not for you to see her tears
When you never even heard her cries

You don't know her walk
You're just someone who likes to talk
If you had to wear her shoes
Would you be able to pay her dues
Talk is cheap; just like your words
One day you'll be wishing your walk was heard

Homeless…will work for food
But, you keep on passing him by
Can't stand to see a grown man
With such an alibi
You've never heard his story about
How for freedom he was willing to die
It's just taken for granted that
Others are trading in their souls for you and I

You don't know his walk
You're just someone who likes to talk
If you had to walk in his shoes
Would you be able to pay his dues

Hunni Bunn

Talk is cheap; just like your words
One day you'll be wishing your walk was heard

Light-skinned and fat
Been hurt every time she tries
Learning about this thing called love
With the different men who lie
And find pleasure in her
By having their nature rise
In the night and by day
Becoming a woman others despise

You don't know my walk
You're just someone who likes to talk
If you had to walk in my shoes
Would you be able to pay my dues
Talk is cheap; just like your words
One day you'll be wishing your walk was heard

LORD, I'm on the Run

LORD, take care of me
Until I am set free
To rest in your arms
Don't allow the world to worry me
Because of what they see
Tell them they can do me no harm

LORD, stretch out your hands to me
Let them part like the Red Sea
Conquer Pharaoh's army
That has been sent after me

My eyes remain on you
No matter what I am going through
My GOD, ALMIGHTY, is strong
When I feel like letting go
Because the pain is starting to show
You give me the strength to hold on

LORD, stretch out your hands to me
Let them part like the Red Sea
Conquer Pharaoh's army
That has been sent after me

My friends may come against me
And of course, family will flee
As the enemy begins to surge
I will have no fear
Because I know you are near

Hunni Bunn

And your glory will emerge

LORD, stretch out your hands to me
Let them part like the Red Sea
Conquer Pharaoh's army
That has been sent after me

22

Soul Journey

There is a place I have to be
GOD has deemed it my destiny
Mankind may focus on what they see
Always wanting to question my mentality
But I'm only doing what I feel is right
Separating the darkness from my light

Soul journey...journey solely for me
Walking what I'm talking
Talking what I'm walking
Soul journey...a journey design to set me free
Walking what I'm talking
Talking what I'm walking
Soul journey...a journey solely for me

You can move one way
While I decide to stay
Wherever it is I decide to be
It's not for you to worry
Just so long as I stay alive
Trust me, I'll find a way to survive

Soul journey...journey solely for me
Walking what I'm talking
Talking what I'm walking
Soul journey...a journey design to set me free
Walking what I'm talking
Talking what I'm walking
Soul journey...a journey solely for me

Yes, satan stays on the loose
Because he can't stand what I produce

Don't want any goodness spreaded
That's why the world is charging so much for
unleaded
Don't think I'm willing to walk it
But, I have to if I'm going to talk it

Soul journey…journey solely for me
Walking what I'm talking
Talking what I'm walking
Soul journey…a journey design to set me free
Walking what I'm talking
Talking what I'm walking
Soul journey…a journey solely for me

My Father's Legacy

There's no tear that could ever fall
Without the failure to make me recall
A friend I met along the way
One who eventually could not stay
And you left me to have it all
When you heard your FATHER's call

Words were weapons when you could hear them
But peace became yours when the way grew dim
We've all had our sins to bear
And mine became so easy with you standing there
Cared enough not to leave me in despair
Nowadays I'm wishing you were back here

If time could even the playing field
Then no heads would need to be healed
For we would keep every man
And Earth would be the Promise Land
But, GOD knows you needed the rest
That's why He only reclaimed the best

Headed for glory
You left the world to tell your story
Some will tell it one way
While others feel you still have a debt to pay
But, I say, if we still love you
Then you've done all that you've had to do

I'm Not Yours

Too many men
For your taste
When it comes to gettin' them in and out
You don't like my haste
Think I'm wrecking too many homes
By allowing so many to become my waste
But sugar, love ain't never been my kind of glue
And permanent ain't never been my type of paste

I might be a hoe
But I'm not your hoe
So, don't ever criticize a place
That you will never get a chance to go

Spending my money
Wasting my dime
On hair, toes, nails and clothes
So, that I may look sublime
To attract the kind of men
Who live off of other men's rhyme
You find no pleasure in it
Saying females like me are just a waste of time

I might be a fool
But I'm not your fool
Street degrees weren't just a requirement
For those who came from the old school

Tricks of the trade
Leave beds unmade

40 Years in the Wilderness

Women upset at the fact
They've been played
Men wanting more
Even offering some up in trade
But I'm the only one who'll make the decision
As to when my body gets laid

I might be a bitch
But I'm not your bitch
Don't call me outside of my name
Just because I don't like the way your balls are pitched

I might be a good-for-nothing
So-and-so to you
But to someone else I am their everything
Because of what I choose to do
I am not what you call me
I am what I answer to
I am not yours
So unto me, my lifestyle will always be true

Printed Panties

Hurt knows every heart
And it certainly has visited mine
The night I allowed you to enter me
And rip out my spine
I told myself
Love is not for you
In darkness sex becomes
Something just to do
Nothing owed
To either lover
Nothing between us
But the covers
Feel free to leave
When the act is done
And if love comes after you
Run baby, run
But I wasn't fast enough
Love caught up with me
Before I could slide back on
My printed panties
My flesh became tainted
My soul pierced
My mental caved in
Knowing I was no longer fierce
My roar has soften
With its need for you
And the knowledge that
I was simply something for you to do
Love will never be obtained
When freely given away

For I offered it without conditions
Under which you'd have to stay
And you remained true
To the act that had taken place
By donning on your clothes
Before I could even plead my case
And now I find myself guilty
Of being painfully aware
If you play with love long enough
Eventually, you'll end up in its snare

Such Is Life

The pain has always
Through the years been there
And down through the years
It has proven to me it's going nowhere

If I rise
It will come along too
Sit back in a corner
And whisper yoo-hoo
You can run
But with all your money
You still can't hide
Now isn't that funny???

If I fall
It will come tumbling down with me
Seven times harder
Than I ever thought it could be
For misery loves company
And pain won't make a sound
But it will be right there with me
Even when others stop coming around

And if I decide to
Stay right here
Rain will have no problem
Pulling up a chair very near
It will allow me a few cheers
But my joy, it will eventually steal
For it is an emotion that survives

40 Years in the Wilderness

Only according to how others feel

Pain has always
Through the years been here
And down through the years
It has proven to me it ain't going nowhere

I Am Beautiful

I am beautiful
No matter what you see
I am beautiful
Because I am happy to be me
I am beautiful
No matter what you see

Glamour!!!
By those who decide
If you don't look a certain way
Then you need to hide
But, I won't let ignorance
Steal away my pride
I was created to enhance
The scenery of this ride
We call life
And yes, I refuse to hide

I am beautiful
No matter what you see
I am beautiful
Because I am happy to be me
I am beautiful
No matter what you see

You can be thin
But never too big
Because if you are
You'll never get a good gig

40 Years in the Wilderness

Many have faltered on their own souls
Just so they look like a twig
That's the lie they try to get me to buy
But, I'm always gone be me, ya dig???

I am beautiful
No matter what you see
I am beautiful
Because I am happy to be me
I am beautiful
No matter what you see

Too short
Never too tall
But the higher you are
The harder you fall
Smoke screens and mirrors
Life isn't always a ball
Even for those who seem
To have it all

I am beautiful
No matter what you see
I am beautiful
Because I am happy to be me
I am beautiful
No matter what you see

I Have Known Love

I have known love
The kind that shows up by day
And into the night
Will gladly stay
Wanting to hold me
In its arms
Wrap me up in the security
That the world will do me no harm
Kiss the corners of my mouth
And then my eyes
Taking the time to enjoy the taste of me
Long before it finds its way between my thighs
Then tenderly it engulfs me
Taking me to a level of love unknown
Passionately, entering and existing me
As if I was an heir to a throne
Meshing our bodies together
Until our fluids escape
Leaving us both breathless
As our mouths stand agape
And even when it's all over
In keeping with the rhythm of the night
Love rolls over next to me
And wrap me in its arms real tight
Enjoying the unison
Of our heartbeats
Never once does it contemplate
Wanting to retreat
But that's not what your love does
You get in and get out

40 Years in the Wilderness

And in between times
Tosses me haphazardly about
Arriving in the morning time
Well after one
And making sure you are gone
Before the rising of the sun
Never once inviting me into your arms
Just to hold me
For that would give me the wrong idea
In you not wanting to be free
Kisses never shared intimately
As to never imply
There will ever be
A chance for you and I
Still, my heart has chosen to love you
Although it won't reveal why
My mental state has even come to know
There will never be a you and I
For I have known love
And all that it can do
Which brings me to the painful conclusion
True love could never be with you

Sticks and Stones

Those words are meant for me
And yes, my heart did hear them
It might have caused the light in it to flicker
But it never did dim
People often make statements
To keep others in a certain place
To keep them off of their game
And out of the race
But, we should never falter
Nor should we bend
Because those tongue thrashers
Will get theirs in the end
They want to throw their weight around
As if they have all the power
But, if you use your tongue to call on GOD too
He'll answer you in your darkest hour
So, let their tongues turn into swords
Prepared to kill the human spirit
And GOD will hold them accountable
For trying to dim the heart His light has lit

No weapon formed against me shall prosper
No matter who with them may concur

Be of Good Cheer

The sky may be falling
Friends may have stopped calling
And family has simply turned away
It might seem easier having a life withdrawal
Than it is for a baby to crawl
Yet, remember, bad times will not stay

Be of good cheer
Knowing that you don't have long to be here
Be of good cheer
The time will come when you can cast away your fear

Tears may rain on your parade
Any others may never come to your aid
Still, keep your soul prayed up
It may seem easier to run away
Than it is for a sinner to pray
Yet, remember, you're not the only one drinking from
a bitter cup

Be of good cheer
Knowing that you don't have long to be here
Be of good cheer
The time will come when you can cast away your fear

Your tongue may become tied
Your aching feet may long for a ride
As others pass you by
It might seem easier just to lie down and die

Than it is for a grown man to cry
Yet, remember, to make it in you've got to try

Be of good cheer
Knowing that you don't have long to be here
Be of good cheer
The time will come when you can cast away your fear

A High-Minded Hoe

Something from nothing
That's where you came from
Now you've gotten a different swag
Since you are dancing to a different drum

Thinking you are about that life
Of credit cards, bottles and labels
It's satellite TV for you now
Forget about cable

Nothing but the best for you
Will now do
Even got a new class of friends
And put down your old crew

Ignoring familiar faces
With a dismissive wave
If they happen to notice you
Like your are something for them to crave

But, just awhile ago
You were living with them
Life on the poor side of town
Didn't seem so grim

It was always
Let's make it together
And you know you're going to be
My girlfriend forever

Hunni Bunn

My, oh my, how we have forgotten
Where we came from
Since we've started
Dancing to a different drum

But, be careful
And do not step on a crack
Because one slip-up
And they are going to send your broke a** back

Run With Myself

I've got the goods
Everybody can see that
Still they don't want
To call me up to bat
They just want to place me on a shelf
Sometimes I have to run with myself

They fear what they can't control
The power is within me
They know I'd rectify many situations
If ever I was set free
So, they want to place me on a shelf
That's why I chose to run with myself

I'm a threat to their very nature
For the façade is there
And I can pull back the covers
And leave their sins bare
So, they want to place me on a shelf
That's why I choose to run with myself

They try to dumb me down
Then call me out
Because they don't want others
To hear my shout
I wasn't built for a shelf
Sometimes I must run with myself

Same Page

No elevation
Just levitation
Done got the master in you
Since we've left the plantation
The same old score
Talking about you can do so much more
--WAIT!!! Isn't this the same page as before
Got me headed
In all different directions
Seeking out what you deem
Pure satisfaction
Trying to score
When life can offer you so much more
--WAIT!!! Isn't this the same page as before
Tinted windows
Brick houses
Rocking scarlet letters
As if we have spouses
Tossing stones to even up the score
Saying we're all in this together once more
But WAIT!!! Isn't this the same page as before
Fingers point
Casting doubt
Off of the one
Who said they'd bring us out
Everyone is taking score
But blaming everyone else once more
--WAIT!!! Haven't we been on this page before
A page turner
Has become a page learner

40 Years in the Wilderness

To avoid
The back burner
Now that I'm keeping my own score
I don't have to say it anymore
Headed in a different direction than I've been before

Here

I woke up with
The sunshine upon my face
The smile of a new day
That I cannot erase
I get to try again
I might even cry again
But, I'm still here
Regardless of what my heart may fear
I'm still here

Morning cups of coffee
Cannot awake me
If there was a shifting of the Earth
It could not shake me
To the presence of a new day
Only the LORD could have His way
To keep me here
Regardless of who may be near
It is He alone who keeps me here

It was grace and mercy
That opened my eye lids
It was forgiveness
That removed the wrongs that yesterday did
And it is with blessings
That a new day began with no stressing
I am no longer here
Therefore, there will be no shedding of tears
For I am still here

Hunni

Hunni!!!
How sweet the flow
That will come from a place
Few people will ever know

My sins speak louder than me
Not because I am the only one
Just that I won't hide
What was not seen by a setting sun

People will not stand poised
Waiting for the proper time to applaud
Even with my credentials
They will point and say fraud

They will only seek out
What could possibly hinder me
For they know my story
Will set the multitude free

And I will say about the good
And yes, even the bad
Life *is* about living
As such it's been the best time I've had

The blues…the booze and yes
Even the unsolicited sex
The bumbling…and fumbling
And the ill-joy of what's next

Mixed in with prayers to GOD
No sooner than I'm brought out
Let me do it again
Because good time living is what I'm all about

They will miss the point
That there was a purpose to it all
In knowing where I have been
I will know how to pick up others who may fall

Hunni!!!
Oh, how sweet the flow
When others stand beside me
They'll never be able to say they didn't know

Karma

There she is
In all of her stubborn glory
Perch right atop my doorstep
Waiting
Poised
Anticipating
That I've forgotten her arrival date
Pouty lips
Hands on hips
Looking like she's finally had enough
Her twisted soul
Is now on fire
I can see its flaming glow
A piece of fiery-red coal
Yet, so cold-hearted is she
That she refuses to pass me by
I want to hop out
The backseat of my cab
Fare in hand
And shake it in front of her face
Yell to her
"See, I've paid my dues!!!"
But, this gesture won't faze her
It's never been about the money
At least when it comes to her
She's the pied-piper of souls
Collecting on seeds
Greed most likely sewn

Hunni Bunn

No amount of money
Can buy her off
My time has come
360° later
She has arrived
And I must allow her will to be so
She doesn't care about my changes
My new attitude
My repentance
My forgiveness
She cares about the old me
The one who has
Been there
Done that
So, with no escape route
Nowhere to run
Nowhere to hide
I walk straight up to her
Stone-faced and all
I extend my hand
To greet her well-manicured fingertips
And offer her a smirk of some kind
She never weakens
She never once bends her lips to smile
I stand poised
Ready
Come what may
"So, you're Karma???"
Still
No response
I continue
"So, we finally meet???"
Her eyes almost pity me

But her lips tell me she won't
They never change
Just as pouty as ever
I waste no more time
In trying to penetrate her icy heart

With the warmth of my touch
I harden my heart
To let her know
I will be going toe-to-toe with her today
I release her hand
A scowl now upon my face
My lifeless lips
Become tout too
As I prepare to finish with her introduction
I become soulless
With lips quivering, I conclude
With words everyone always uses
"I heard you were a bit**…"
She doesn't even flinch
Not shocked at all
I'm quite sure she's heard those words before
But
Never
Has she heard the ones to follow
I go into my fighting stance
Fists balled up
Feet planted
"Well, so am I," I say
"Life made me that way.
Are you ready for the fight of your life???
If so, let the games begin!!!"

Life's a mother…
I'm so glad I was born a female, too
Knowing that she bleeds just like me
Karma will forever remember my name

Let's get it on!!!

Will You Be There???

In my down-time
When my wings will not propel me to fly
Will you be the one
To hear my cry

Will you see me
Swamped in hurt
Pain radiating my mind
Do to others being so curt

Will you remember my name
Like memories from yesterday
When we were innocent
Only looking for kiddie-games to play

In all those years Red Rover
Never sent anyone right over
Even when I wasn't looking for
Anything more than a lover

Will you remember my heart
Before my blood became blue
Will you fictionalize all my beliefs
By telling me they were never true

So, that I may continue on this journey
In believing nothing is as it seems
And that all this hurt is imagined

Because life is but a dream

Will you lift me up
Will you restore me to my former glory
Will you give me a beautiful ending
To this fairy-tale story

As my friend
As my family
As my reason
For being me

In my darkest hour
When I am sinking in deep despair
Having known me before
My heart asks the question will you be there

Will you offer me a hand
Will you still refer to me as friend
Or will you walk on by
Never to recognize me again

Will you be there???

Splintered

Time changes all things
Even when we believe in forever
For no two things in this world
Can share an eternity together

We can love hard and play nicely
We can even laugh out loud
But, on the horizon
There will always be a hint of a gray cloud

Winds will blow
And the rains will fall
And yes, a friend may weather a few storms
But, will never always be on call

We'll bask in the glory
On most sunny days
Then we'll stowaway
When the skies turn gray

Never take it personal
That the one you thought would always be near
Will be the first to turn and run
At sight of the first tear

So, never hold onto anything too tight
Unless it leaves splinters in your heart
Life has no permanent cast members
Only actors and actresses playing their parts

In Remembrance of Sammy Isley, Jr.
(Daddy)

Baby girl woke up to the news this morning
That you had gone
Had to take a final trip
And this time you had to go it alone
No time was there
For saying good-bye
You'll never get to see
All the tears I'll now cry

Daddy, may you rest in peace
Loved me until time had to cease
So, I'll treasure the memories we shared together
Until the time that we'll be able to share forever

Always working hard
For things that never cost a dime
Just waiting on the day
When you could find the time
To rest your weary mind
And enjoy what was left in life
A moment when the winds had calmed
No longer offering you stress and strife

Daddy, may you rest in peace
Loved me until time had to cease
So, I'll treasure the memories we shared together
Until the time that we'll be able to share forever

Life has been rearranged

40 Years in the Wilderness

With no certainty of tomorrow
Yes, I have to be real careful
Not to carry with me any sorrow
Even if on some days
Someone else's smile I have to borrow
I have to accept the fact daddy's gone on
Still, I will always love him so

Daddy, may you rest in peace
Loved me until time had to cease
So, I'll treasure the memories we shared together
Until the time that we'll be able to share forever

Blessed

When there is no understanding
To what you are going through
When you wake up to find
A sun that can show you nothing new
The easiest thing to do
Is to climb back inside of your mind
And curse the day
You ever became a part of mankind

When your smile contradicts
What your heart is feeling
And you become numb
Due to the joy others are stealing
The easiest thing to do
Is to climb back into your shell
And contemplate trading heaven
For an eternity in hell

When death becomes more enticing
Than life does
When you think about all that has been
And you wish it never was
The easiest thing to do
Is to make time stand still
You think to yourself
I can't hurt if I can't feel

When tomorrow doesn't look promising
And your heart no longer cares to go on
When your cries have turned into

40 Years in the Wilderness

Nothing more than painful moans
The easiest thing to do
Is to drop down on your knees and pray
For there is truly a blessing in the fact
That GOD allowed you to see another day

Call Him

Call Him
In the midnight hour
When the world feels like
It's you it can so easily devour
Let Him be your comforter
As He wraps His arms around you
Let Him be your protector
For He'll surely see you through

Call Him
King of your home
His kind of love
Won't allow you to roam
Looking for a man
Who's not dedicated to you
He'll praise you for your virtue
When others don't give you your just due

Call Him
Without spending one dime
He's available 24/7
That's right...at any given time
He'll never hang up on you
He'll never deny your call
And when you feel like giving up
He'll catch you before you can fall

Call Him
A provider...conqueror...even best friend
For He'll be right there

40 Years in the Wilderness

When others won't let you in
He'll stick closer than a brother
And love you more than your mother
If you just trust in Him
You will need to lean on no other

Call Him…GOD!!!

Call Him!!!
Call Him!!!
Call Him…GOD!!!

Call Him!!!
Call Him!!!
Call Him…LORD of lords

Call Him…He's waiting to hear from you, right now!!!

The Stillness

The rising…
And the falling of your chest
Stilled by the knowledge
GOD has taken away the best
No more understandable chats
No more understanding of me
My best friend has had to move on
In order for me to fly free
As pain eludes your body
And your eyelids close for the very last time
I rest on the knowledge
You could not have stayed even if I'd given my very
last dime
I have to live with my memories of love
And goodwill I have shown you
During my walk in your lifetime
If peace is to ensue
The opening of a new day
Serves as a reminder you will no longer be joining me
Yes, our Father has called you home
And I have to accept that reality
In the stillness so many refers to as peace
There is no room for compromising
For many will have to go to sleep as such
In order to enjoy that great Day of rising

Me

No more tears today
I gave them all away
Yes, my heart has grown
And is telling me it's time to move on
To include me
In everything I desire to be

No more dancing for others
No more trying to be another
Because people choose not to love me
Simply because they don't like what they see
Still it's all in me
To be whom I desire to be

Only I can set free
The hurt inside of me
Fill my heart up with glory
By embracing my story
My journey had to be long
In order for me to become strong

I tried to please this world
That's when my life unfurled
No longer a gift to me
Until I was made to see
I wasn't designed to be
Anything other than me

JESUS

When the world is
Pointing its finger at you
Like you owe it something
And the bill has come due
And it won't receive
What you have to give
Still with nothing
It expects for you to live

JESUS—call Him
JESUS—call Him
JESUS—call Him
He'll hear you
And yes, He'll see you through

When you are down
And feel like you can't get up
When you are used to half
And now empty is your cup
And you need some rejuvenation
From the way this world spins
Don't count on others
But, know on Him, you can depend

JESUS—call Him
JESUS—call Him
JESUS—call Him
He'll hear you
And yes, He'll see you through

40 Years in the Wilderness

When you have done
All that you know to do
And you feel like
You won't make it through
Call on JESUS
And never ever give into doubt
No matter your situation
He has the power to bring you out

JESUS—call Him
JESUS—call Him
JESUS—call Him
He'll hear you
And yes, He'll see you through

Victorious

No man knows the road
On which you have traveled
So, do not hand over your victory to them
In which they may unravel
Your passions
Your dreams
For many may cheer you on
But, in reality, may not be on your team
There is victory
In being knocked down
For it takes courage and determination
To turn defeat around
Your walk may not be
Their walk
Your talk may not be
Their talk
But all the same
You are still here
So, hide not behind the scene
Out of fear
You have the right to exist
For you have your own destiny
God is the only watcher to be concerned with
But, for everybody else say, see me!!!
The one you counted out
The one you thought would never shine
Well, GOD has smiled down on me today
And said, "Victory is mine…"
Take up your burdens
And get to walking this road again

For you are the only one who can determine
How the world should embrace your sins

Victory is mine
Victory is mine
Victory today is mine
I told satan
Get thee behind
VVVIIICCCTTTOOORRRYYY
Today is mine!!!

Divine DYVA

A fantasy
Given life
At a time when
My heart was filled with strife
A little girl
Born of me
Leaving questions
Concerning her beauty
And I smile
Knowing you belong to me
Whom GOD has deemed worthy
To others will always remain a mystery
You were given to me
As an attempt to save my soul
And GOD knowing no failure
Knew this act of love has made me whole
I have chosen better
In order to do right by you
For you are of my flesh
And watching what it is I do
So, in your name, I proclaim
I am mother
To a true diva indeed
And wouldn't want any other
Because no matter
What you take me through
GOD saw a reason
To give me you
A blessing and
An original design
For me to mold and return to Him
Even more refined

Real Man

You thought you had me
At I love you
You thought I would be blind
To all the things you'd do
But I looked around
And found a different source
To entrust my heart to
And place me on a different course
Of satisfaction
When I was in need
Without the outside world
Having to intercede
To make him a better man
For on virtue and wisdom
He'll always stand
No more feeling like
I owe Him more than He's giving
No more being scrutinized
About the way I'm living
With threats of dismissal
If I don't go along with His game
And He also gave me understanding
That bit** is not my name
So, guess what???
I'm the one who gets to walk away
With no more threats
About my life ending in disarray
Because you thought
I couldn't make it without you

But when you left a real man showed up
And said, "It's time for me to show you what I can
do."
He lifted me out of this world of despair
With the words, if you'll have me, I'll always be there
I'll supply all your needs
Because that's how much I really care
So, I put down all the burdens you left me with
And allowed this Man to make me whole
All these years I was trying to love the wrong man
When it was GOD who deserved my mind, body and
soul

Redeemed

Trials
Tribulation
Everything going wrong
With no jubilation

Sometimes we want to
Sit on down
Sometimes our smiles
Turn into frowns

We don't think we can make it
This world has gone awry
We forget to look towards the heavens
In order to be inspired

GOD has a plan for everybody
And yes, it includes you
For the day He created man
He gave us all something productive to do

Most of us have absconded
Our role in this life
Because we became overwhelmed
With stress and strife

We let our knees buckle
And our hearts grow cold
By looking back on mistakes
That GOD has considered old

Hunni Bunn

We've got to get back
To where we started from
Knowing that GOD has gifted us
With every tool needed to overcome

So, quit harping on
What's already been done
And let's look at life everyday as
A race that can still be won

Trials
Tribulations
That's just apart
Of every generation

Don't give in
Don't give up
Go even harder
When bitter is the cup

Forty Years in the Wilderness

Woe unto me
The woman you see
Captivating
Mesmerizing
Having been set free
To be…simply, to be

Forty-years in the wilderness
And He cleaned up this mess
Forty-years in the wilderness
Made me a witness
Forty-years that I was blessed
In coming out of the wilderness

Heavy-hearted and always broken
Looking for words unspoken
Crazy mind
And fleshy-fine
Always somebody's love token

Forty-years in the wilderness
And He cleaned up this mess
Forty-years in the wilderness
Made me a witness
Forty-years that I was blessed
In coming out of the wilderness

Mankind never been so kind

Hunni Bunn

When it came to this heavenly find
Torrid
And spent
Is when I made up my mind

Forty-years in the wilderness
And He cleaned up this mess
Forty-years in the wilderness
Made me a witness
Forty-years that I was blessed
In coming out of the wilderness

No more to abhor
Nothing more to live for
This diamond in the rough
Has had enough
Gone try a different door

Forty-years in the wilderness
And He cleaned up this mess
Forty-years in the wilderness
Made me a witness
Forty-years that I was blessed
In coming out of the wilderness

Forty-years were way too long~~~
But, thank GOD, it made this back right here real
strong~~~

Prayer Kept Me

I cannot tell a lie
Nor am I looking for an alibi
For GOD has kept me
Even when I was in iniquity
Lost; thinking I was doing good
Because I was in a place I misunderstood
Looking for highs
By embracing lies
Oh, you are a pretty girl
Oh, you belong to this world
Turn it up
And pass me my cup
Drank many a bitter drink
Because it controlled the way I think
And the world was alright with me
Because I was allowed to be free
I gave in
To many more sins
Like the pleasures of men
Who would only pretend
To love me
Just to invade my body
Then one day
A voice told me to turn from my wicked ways
Thus, giving me a brand new song
That I can sing all the day long
Yes, while even in sin
And until its end
When I desired to be set free
It was prayers of others that kept me

Hunni Bunn

Redemption

Wretched, raggedy
A hot-a**-mess
Born beyond sin
That's why I stress
Clawing and climbing
With nowhere to be
Wouldn't accept a blessing
If it included parting the Red Sea
Singing and dancing
Gyrating my soul
Glad to have on-lookers
Because I felt like I had control
Death, dying
My world came to an end
Thank GOD for second chances
In letting a new one begin

How High

How high
Can I fly
Some say
Not too high
And those who do
I say bye
Don't tell me
That lie
For my dreams
Reach beyond the sky
And I'm going to soar
If I just give it a try
So, don't try
To limit how high
I can
Truly fly
For my dreams
Reach far beyond the sky

360°

I woke up on
The other side of life
And looked back with fondness
On all my past stress and strife
Reasons for it all
To tell others I've been there
I may not know your walk
But sometimes my feet too, have been bare
I've been unclothed
In the acts of sin
Ain't no use in me lying
Or trying to pretend
I don't have a past
I don't know what it's like to do wrong
For all that I've been through
Is what has made me strong
My purpose was revealed to me
Due to the fact I allowed myself to fall
And now I have a reason
To embrace it all
I've made it over
By allowing my mind and heart to align
My days may bring the same challenges
The difference—I know I'm going to be just fine

The Quick Fix

I could tell you all
That I didn't know me
And you would think
I was lying
I, myself, would have to question
The logic in that statement
If I didn't have the heart to know
I was telling the truth
In that I know I want happiness
But, I seek out joy in places
That only offer it artificially
I know already how it's going
To come…and go…just as fast
As it came
Still, I will seek it out
Because that's the only way
I know how to get it
My mind says No!
My heart says Yes!
And in-between I meet
Heaven and hell
I love the moments
When I truly hate myself
Because I am giving into something
That truly doesn't love me back
Simply because it makes me feel
So…so…good
And then it's gone
I want to break the cycle

But, I've already told you
I don't know how
Because I truly don't know myself
That's my reality
That's my story
Finding pleasure in places
Where there truly is none
Addictions…

The Promise of Tomorrow

Nothing sweeter than the sorrow
Of having to face another tomorrow
Even in knowing that yesterday is done
There's a joy in knowing fate hasn't won
Second chances are often denied
To those who are unaware as they lay sleepy-eyed
Dreams may dance about the head
Yet, for some, time made the hour their cooling bed
Can't catch yesterday's rainbows
The what ifs permanently becomes the I don't knows
Actions solidify memories that will last
As love ones recall the past
Good or bad, it's all left unfinished
Only the soul left behind to be replenished
And we think we have another day
To do what we do; to say what we say
Always in the back of our minds
That additional time won't be hard to find
Then with the twinkling of the eye
Someone says good-bye
And we understand
We're only a part of a greater plan
Eventually, we must all experience that rift
That's why the present is a gift
To give to others good deeds
As we sow our Earthly seeds
Don't ever rest on the fact
That you'll be given a second chance to react

For yesterday can't be undone
And as for tomorrow, fate may have won
And today could become that final moment
Of how well your life was spent
Therefore, love, laugh and above all…live!
For the promise of tomorrow is not yours to give

Bitter Cup

Generations it came across
That all souls would be lost
If we didn't stop to add up the cost
Remembering in bearing the cross
GOD's love manifested itself
By saying none would be left
If we just believe
And, in quest for salvation, receive
His Holy Commandments to do what's right
That's why His Son was born one starry night
To take away our sins
So, that one day we may live again
In peace, so serene
A divine mansion to change the scene
Bricks of gold to pave the way
With no more debts to pay
A crown of thorns tell the story
Of how we inherited His glory
Pierced in His side
For having nothing to hide
An innocent man resigned to His fate
Thirty pieces of silver was the going rate
To put our salvation on the line
For the redemption of all mankind
Yet, what a bitter cup it must have been for Him to swallow
That as our Savior, it's Him whom we do not follow

Late in the Midnight Hour

In the midnight hour
I turn out the lights
To welcome the darkness
That will restore my sight
I go down on my knees
In a position that is sure to please
Done in a fashion
So, no one else sees
I draw on all the wetness
In my mouth
For it will surely be dry
By the time I rise again from the South
I clasp my hands together
With pressure to me yet unknown
For as time grows longer
I'll feel the strength of the seeds I've sewn
With head bowed
I begin to call on your name
Knowing after tonight
My life will never be the same
JESUS...JESUS...JESUS
Who strengthens me
Take time out to hear my prayer request
That I be made free
From burdens, pain and misery
Let all weapons prove useless
Knowing that I am a child of GOD
I bring to you all my stress
So, that through the night
May my body and mind find rest

40 Years in the Wilderness

And in the morning I'll be renewed
To overcome all of life's little tests
Because I serve a mighty GOD
And yes, I am speaking of You
For I know what You can do
My GOD is able and will bring me on through
In the midnight hour
When I can't see the light
GOD is working it out for me
And I know everything is going to be alright

Hunni Bunn

In My Darkest Hour

Now Mary came a-running
Saying her brother was sick in bed
JESUS came a-walking
For four days Lazarus had been dead
Now they didn't know exactly what GOD could do
Until JESUS breathe life into Lazarus anew

In my darkest hour
I know what my GOD can do
Even in the darkness
He will bring me through

Now an issue dealing with blood arose
After this lady went
To every doctor she could go to
Until all of her money was spent
They still couldn't cure her
Leaving her without once red cent
Until she was able to touch the hem of JESUS's
garment
And out of her the issue went

In my darkest hour
I know what my GOD can do
Even in the darkness
He will bring me through

Now there was a multitude
Five-thousand was the count
The people didn't have enough food
To feed such a massive amount

40 Years in the Wilderness

Then JESUS said bring me what you do have
That was five fishes and two loaves of bread
And it was through Him with such a small amount
All those people were fed

In my darkest hour
I know what my GOD can do
Even in the darkness
He will bring me through

Free Me

Broke…
Broken…
For me
That's what my life's been

Hurt
Haunted
By a past
That's always taunted

Nothing
Nonetheless
Born into iniquity
So, I've never been blessed

And I stumble
Sometimes I even fall
But thank GOD
On You, I never forgot to call

So, I'm calling on You
Right now, in Your name
Release me from this mental prison
In which I accept all the blame

Crying

Oh Savior, my GOD
Can you hear my humble cry
As I go through this life
Please be there to draw me nigh
I am trying to make it
But, it's not so easy at all
So, if the time should ever come
Please, do not let me fall

Can you hear me crying
Crying out to you
Yes, I'm crying, crying
Do not let the pain ensue
My GOD, do whatever it is
You have to do

Mountains galore
In places I've never been before
Don't know which way to go
Because I can't take it anymore
My walk has grown weary
My legs no longer desire to stand
For it feels like time is sinking
Like an hourglass low on sand

Can you hear me crying
Crying out to you
Yes, I'm crying, crying
Do not let the pain ensue

My GOD, do whatever it is
You have to do

My journey may never be finished
Before I meet my end
But, GOD almighty, in the meantime
Send me all the mercy you have to send
Embrace me with grace and understanding
That this race can be won
For You made it so
When You gave us Your only begotten Son

Can you hear me crying
Crying out to you
Yes, I'm crying, crying
Do not let the pain ensue
My GOD, do whatever it is
You have to do

I've Been Here All the While

You were out searching
Looking for someone to care
You were looking high and low
Looking just about everywhere
No sleep for a restless heart
One with no love to share
For a life without someone to love
Is a life no one wants to bear

Running to and fro
Knowing not where to go
For love was eluding you
When it came time to be true
Just when you felt you'd gone your final mile
You realized I've been here all the while

Pain had you crying
Ready to walk away
Got you looking at your own self funny
As to why no one would stay
Lost in a sea of turmoil
Hopelessly locked in a world of despair
Just when you were about to give up
Love showed you it had always been there

Running to and fro
Knowing not where to go
For love was eluding you
When it came time to be true

Just when you felt you'd gone your final mile
You realized I've been here all the while

Change ain't never been easy
When you are so used to losing
Especially when you are playing
A game not of your choosing
Love often offers you these crazy chances
Leaving your heart in a spin
But it's often the choice you've never thought to make
In which you will win

Running to and fro
Knowing not where to go
For love was eluding you
When it came time to be true
Just when you felt you'd gone your final mile
You realized I've been here all the while

About the Author

Hunni Bunn resides in North Carolina where she spends most of her days enjoying single parenthood with her daughter Dyva. She has a B.S. Degree in Communications. She is the last of eight siblings. Although she may bend, she will never break. Her goal in life is to fully utilize her gift by being a living testimony to GOD who granted her the ability to pen such wonderful, meaningful works that will ultimately impact other people's lives in a positive way. Forty Years in the Wilderness chronicles her life's journey out of obscurity into a life of light.